Edmund "Hoot" Sauls has written a tale that will surely remind you of a simpler time and place. This "slice of life" memoir will transport readers back to their younger days and remind them of the small things in life that bring joy and laughter.

—Jeff Jones,
Pastor, First Baptist Church,
Villa Rica

Edmund Sauls
"Hoot"

The
Linthead

— EDMUND "HOOT" SAULS —

The Linthead

TATE PUBLISHING *& Enterprises*

Published by Tate Publishing & Enterprises, LLC
127 E. Trade Center Terrace | Mustang, Oklahoma 73064 USA
1.888.361.9473 | www.tatepublishing.com

Tate Publishing is committed to excellence in the publishing industry. The company reflects the philosophy established by the founders, based on Psalm 68:11,
"The Lord gave the word and great was the company of those who published it."

Book design copyright © 2009 by Tate Publishing, LLC. All rights reserved.
Cover design by Amber Gulilat
Interior design by Nathan Harmony

Published in the United States of America

ISBN: 978-1-61566-592-1
1. Biography & Autobiography: Personal Memoirs
2. Biography & Autobiography: General
09.12.14

Dedication

To my wife Edith.
To my three daughters, Belinda Dianne
Smith, Cathy Susanne Thomas, and
Patricia Gail Chapman.
To the memories of each family that lived
in Fullerville, and to their loved ones.

Preamble

In the 1930s to 1940s, most Southern towns and cities had cotton mills. The textile industry had begun to deteriorate, and there was lots of unemployment, low wages, long hours, night work, and miserable factory conditions. Mill agents controlled these southern mill towns with the company providing jobs, houses, food, clothing, and goods. Inside those mills, the lint from the cotton floated freely in the air. So the nickname *Linthead* was born. A lot of men and women worked all their life in the cotton mill. If you were lucky enough to have started work in the middle to late forties, there was still time to find other means of employment. The cotton mill industry was failing because of international competition, especially from Japan. Experiences of my early boyhood and young manhood are reflected in this book.

The Linthead

I was born in Fullerville, Georgia, which was a small cotton mill village located approximately one mile north of the city of Villa Rica on Highway 101. I was born on the fourth of July in 1930. Back then, doctors would come to your home to see patients and to deliver babies. Those days are gone forever. I was the fifth child of six born into our family. There were three older bothers, one older sister, and one younger brother. Since I was born on the Fourth of July, Mr. Florence put a box in his store for people to put names in to suggest what I should be called. Mama said they almost named me Lyman, after Lyman Hall. To tell you the truth, I am glad I dodged that bullet. I have been called "Hoot" for as long as I can remember. Some say they got the name from Hoot Gibson, the cowboy, but I am not sure of that. My real name is Charles Edmund Sauls.

My dad worked in the cotton mill. He was the master mechanic. He had the responsibility to keep gears and other equipment repaired or replaced. I remember, as a small lad of a boy, I would walk down to the mill and watch him as he worked the big lathe machine. He could make almost anything on that machine. I loved to watch my daddy work. We only lived about a hundred yards from his work place, and even though I was under six years old, I would walk down to the mill as I pleased.

At nighttime, I slept with my daddy, while my youngest brother, Roger, slept with my mama. I really loved my daddy, and everybody said I was his favorite. My older brothers and sister slept on the sleeping porch of the house. It was one of the better mill houses, since my daddy had a job of some importance.

My dad was offered a job at the mill in Tennille, Georgia. It was to pay fifty cents an hour more, and he thought, since he had such a large family, it would be a good move. We moved to Tennille, Georgia, and as it turned out, he was never happy with the job. After a short stay of a year or less, he took his job back at the Fullerville Mill. When we moved back to Villa Rica, we had a house just across from the Villa Rica Grammar School.

One afternoon, as I sat in my daddy's lap on the front porch of that house, he said, "You start to school this year, don't you?"

I said, "Yes sir."

He said to me, "Well, I will buy you a bicycle when you do."

Sorry to say he never got the opportunity to buy the bicycle, because he developed pneumonia in both lungs and died before I reached my sixth birthday. The only medicine to treat his condition was sulfur drugs, and they did not do the job. Later, penicillin was discovered and was more affective for that type of illness.

After my daddy died, my oldest brother Curtis was the only one in our family who could work. He was given a supervisor job in the cotton mill, so we had to move back to Fullerville, into one of the mill houses. Cecil later would take a job in the cotton mill, and James would take a job in the hosiery mill. We survived in the days of the depression.

There was a school in Fullerville, which went from the first through the third grade. That was where I started in the first grade. Mrs. Henderson was the teacher for all three grades. The school had one large room, where all three grades were located. One of the students, named Curt, was always running away from school. Mrs. Henderson would get busy with other children, and Curt would raise a window and jump out to the ground. He would not be seen any more that day. Mrs. Henderson was a very kind and gentle woman, and I loved her a lot. In one of my classes, I was called on to read from my book. I had a habit of standing with one foot on my desk seat. As I was reading, my weight shifted, and my right knee jammed down behind the seat of my desk. I could not get it to come loose. I was embarrassed and also crying. Mrs. Henderson sent someone to the cotton mill to get help with my problem. Mr. Rast and Fate Barber came with some tools and had to take out some bolts to get my knee out of the desk. I never did that again. After I completed the second grade at the Fullerville School, it was closed down. I entered the third grade at the Villa Rica Grammar School. Ironically, I would have a Miss Henderson for my third grade teacher. She was not related to my first and second grade teacher Mrs. Henderson.

Transferring from grammar school to high school was quite an experience. On the first day of school, it was customary for all the boys to go through the beltline. All the upperclassman would line up outside on both sides of the sidewalk going in and out of the building. They would take their belts off, and all the freshmen were required to run down the sidewalk and take the blows. If you ran really fast, you might get by some of them. There were as always some of them who would try to hit you in the face. If you did not go through the beltline, all the other boys called you "yellow."

At recess time, something was always going on. There were always boxing gloves available. I didn't mind being challenged, as long as it was not too much difference in weight or a much older boy. The school authorities didn't seem to mind this going on. I doubt it would be allowed today. There were two students transferred to our school who had been expelled from Carrollton High School for misconduct. They began to be a problem in our classrooms. Some of the boys decided to log pile them after class. As the two young men walked out on the playground, they went after them. They caught one of them and log piled him there in the yard. The other boy was too fast to catch. He ran, and the last time I saw him he was headed down toward the railroad. Those two boys never came back to our school.

We used to brag to one another that our little village was actually incorporated and on the Georgia map. We were an incorporated town with our own mayor and police. There was a little courthouse with one room, where council meetings were held when needed. We had a cement jail consisting of two rooms, where town drunks were kept until they sobered up. The cement jail is still there today. Fullerville was a textile town consisting of a cotton mill, a hosiery mill and a lumberyard. There was a spur railroad track off of the mainline, which passed onto the lumber mill and was located north of the cotton mill. The track passed over Highway 101, which was a dirt road back then. The cotton mill ran its machinery by power it got from steam boilers. There was a large wheel, about thirty feet in diameter. This wheel was made to rotate by the steam supplied by the boilers. There was a large shaft connected to the wheel, which passed through the center of the mill. This large shaft had pulleys on it at various locations throughout the mill. The machines were connected to these pulleys by two belts so that they could be started and stopped. There were picker rooms, card rooms, spinning rooms, twister rooms, winder rooms, packing rooms, and shipping rooms. The hosiery mill, of course, produced socks. I was not as familiar with the hosiery mill as I was with the cotton mill. I never worked in the hosiery mill, but I had a mother, sister, and brother who did work there.

The cotton mill fired their boilers with coal. The coal was delivered to the mill by rail. Sometime loose coal would fall off the rail cars and onto the railroad. All the mill houses had fireplaces. Most would buy coal to burn, but sometimes they would burn wood. Some folks would walk the railroad with a bucket and pick up the loose pieces of coal, which had fallen off the railcars. Times were hard, and they did the best they could. You could order coal delivered to your house, if you had the money to pay for it. Some of the places in town would sell coal by the sack full.

Most everyone in the village had fireplaces and wood stoves. Kindling wood was in demand at all times. You could find it most of the time in the woods and cut it up in small strips. It would light very easily. Just strike a match and hold it to the wood for a minute, and you would have a fire started. One time, Sam Skinner asked me to get some kindling wood and chop it up for him, and I did. Near the end of the week, I went over to collect my money from him. Now Sam loved to play the fiddle.

When I knocked on the door, Sam was playing his fiddle and could not hear me knocking on the door. I wasn't worried about getting paid, because Sam was a fine and very honest man. I decided not to bother him, so I left and came back later to get my money.

At home we burned what wood we could get. Most of the time, it was cut up into slabs sold by the pickup-load. We were out of wood, and one of the local men that I knew came by with a pickup truck load of wood for sell. Mama asked him if he would let her have it and pay him that weekend when she got her check. He refused to give her the wood and said he did not do any credit. As a young impressionable boy, I never forgot him or the incident. It was later in life, as an adult man, that I looked at him one day and said "Lord, please forgive me for holding a grudge against this man." I immediately felt a peace that I had not had about this man and that situation.

The lumberyard had a planing mill for finished lumber and a saw mill for unfinished lumber. We as boys loved to play on the large piles of sawdust and to hide among the stacks of lumber. The lumber was stacked in such a way to dry that we could climb the stacks of lumber and go down inside the stacks from the top. We would make rubber guns out of a stick, a clothes pin, and strips of rubber cut from inner tubes. We played cowboys and Indians for hours at a time there.

Most all the goods from the cotton mill, the hosiery mill, and the lumber mill were shipped by rail. The cotton mill received coal cars, and their boilers were fired with the coal from the cars. Empty boxcars were left at the loading dock at the cotton mill. This was another source of play for us boys. We would get inside the cars and play as if we were hoboes on a journey. The spur track played an important part in the history of Fullerville.

There were no busses from Fullerville to the school in Villa Rica, so we walked to school. It was a challenge for us boys to see how far we could walk on the rails before we stepped off the track. It was about a mile and a half from Fullerville to the school. The spur track intersected about one hundred yards with the mainline track. After that, we could leave the tracks and walk a dirt street on over to the school.

On the mainline, about three miles out of Villa Rica going west, a freight train had stopped. I do not know why the train was stopped on the mainline, but it was. At one time all freight trains carried a caboose. In the caboose, there was a flagman who performed several duties. We were told that the flagman should have gone to back up the track to warn other trains that they were stopped on the track. For some reason the flagman never left the caboose. A westbound train ran into the train that was stopped on the track. It was a terrible accident. The caboose of the train, which was stopped, was hit with full speed of the engine. Boxcars and other cars were scattered everywhere. As soon as we heard about it, several of us boys walked over to the crash site. If you stooped down and looked under the wreckage, you could see the body of the flagman tangled up in the wreckage. I wished a lot of times that I had never looked under there and saw that sight. I could hear the blowing of the steam engine's whistles all night long, as the workers untangled the mess on the tracks. Even now, these many years later, I can hear the diesel engines blowing their whistles. They do not sound the same as the steam engines. Sometimes when I am restless at night and those diesel engines begin to blow, I use my imagination and pretend I am on a long journey. I still love to hear those whistles. It takes my mind off of things I am thinking about and gives me some comfort to hear their sound.

Another day as I made my way to school, I was about fifty yards from where I would leave the track to go to school. I was walking the rail on the right-hand side. I looked down and there, between the crossties on the track, was the head of a black person. I was frightened out of my wits. The boys on the other side of the tracks began to scream. There on the other side of the tracks was the body. We got word to the school, and they sent someone out to pick up the remains. I could not understand how his head was cut off so smoothly. That was not for me to worry about but for the proper authorities. In the future, bars with bells and lights would be installed at the crossings, but prior to that a number of people would lose their lives at these crossings in Villa Rica. I knew most all of them. My girlfriend Edith (who later became my wife) and I were walking home from the movie, and we saw the excitement near the Marchman house. Someone had been run over by a train at that crossing. Three other men and one young girl would lose their lives at these crossings at a later date.

One of my most entertaining events was when the railroad would send a crew to work on the switch tracks. It was so neat to hear those workmen sing as they would drive those spikes into the crossties. The rails were measured for width, and then a predrilled plate was placed on each side of the rail through which the spikes were driven. Those workmen would line up about ten feet apart, and with their sledge-hammers would sink the spikes. They seemed to never miss a lick. As they drove the spikes, the lead driver would sing out, and in perfect cadence, the other drivers would follow in perfect harmony. I could stay there for hours, watching those men work.

The track split behind Rayford Grubbs barbershop. One set of tracks went toward the lumber mill, and the other went to the cotton mill. We used to go to the switching point and move the switching arm from one position to the other just for fun. The switching tracks would move from one side to another depending on which way you wanted to go. They didn't keep a lock on the switching arm, so it was something for us to play with.

I hated washday. It was my duty to fill three number-two wash tubs and one black wash pot with water, under which a fire was built to heat the water. To do this, water had to be drawn from a well and carried two buckets at a time, until all the tubs were full of water. We shared a well with four or five families. It was a community well, which was about fifty yards from our house. After the clothes boiled for a while, you would take a broom handle and transfer the clothes into the first rinse and so on, until you passed through all the tubs of water. Most of the clothes were then placed in the starch water and then wrung out by hand.

They were then hung out on a clothesline to dry in the sun. The women would do the ironing. The clothes might not have been designer clothes as they have today, but they could put a crease on a pair of pants like you would not believe. My mama could iron a white shirt better than any tailor could. We were poor folks, but we were proud folks. These were hard times in the early thirties and forties.

Mama needed help with her ironing. It was a pretty good job to try to iron for five boys, one daughter, and herself. We had a lady who would come once a week and iron for mama. We didn't have the fancy electric irons they have today. The irons we had would have to be heated on the wood stove in our kitchen, so you needed more than one iron. While you used one iron, the other was heating on the stove. The lady lived on the other side of what we called "Slickum." Slickum was the woods on the west side of Fullerville. We used to rabbit hunt in the woods and would spend many hours there. One week there was no need for the lady to come, and I was told that I had to go and tell her. I don't think Mama realized how close to dark it was. I hurried as best I could. I entered the woods behind the Rast home and proceeded to make my way through the woods. I guess it was about a mile and a half to where she lived. I made it there all right and gave her the message from Mama. As I started back, it had begun to get dusty dark. Before I had gone halfway through the woods toward home, it had become dark. Luckily, there was a moon that night, or I would not have been able to see the path in the woods. Every bush looked like someone was behind it. I was afraid to run, because if someone were there, they would have heard me, and I didn't want to see anyone. I walked as fast as I could, trying to get out of those woods. When I arrived back at Mr. Rast's house, I never was so relieved in my life.

We spent a lot of time in Slickum. There was a cave there. The word was that they tried to find gold in those red hills. All I ever saw was what we called *fools gold*. There was a lot of that. Robert was my best friend. Robert, two other boys who were new in the neighborhood, and I got together and decided to go to Slickum. Once there, we went inside the cave and dug out dirt, which looked like gold, but in reality was only "fool's gold." We also picked up some of the shiny-looking dirt and put it in sacks. Robert and I did not really know the two boys with us that well. If we had, we would never have gone there with them. We returned home with the two sacks of fool's gold and left them at Robert's house. The next day, some of the adults that were there told us the dirt was worthless. Robert and I took the dirt and threw it out. The next day, the two boys saw us playing in the yard. They came up to us in the yard, and I didn't realize it, but they had pocketknives in their hands. They were older boys than Robert and I and were able to control us. They forced us to walk out in the field behind Robert's house. Their knives looked really scary. They said, "We know that you took the gold and threw it down the toilet hole." All the houses had out-house toilets, and that's where they claimed we threw it. I was really fearful for my life. Those knives looked really scary. Finally, they tired of toying with us, and we were allowed to go back to the house. Later in the week, we had a rock battle with them. They were in their yard, and we were in ours. Luckily, no one was hurt. A short time later the mill would fire their parents and ask them to move. I never was so glad to see a family move away.

I spent most of my days playing at Robert's house. His mother, Jewell, would always set a place for me at her table. They had a garden at the back of their house, as most people in the village did. Jewell was working in her garden. One day, Robert and I were playing in a tent he had made next to the house. The tent was situated so that you could crawl under his house from inside the tent. Robert had his air rifle with him. Aunt Pearl lived next door to Robert's house. Jimmy was aunt Pearl's son. He was out back, hanging up clothes on the line in the yard. He was wearing a leather jacket. I saw him there and decided he was a good target for my air rifle. I took aim from inside the tent and fired the air rifle. The shot struck Jimmy in the back of his leather jacket. I know it did not hurt him at that distance, but it made a loud pop. He turned immediately and had an ugly look on his face. He charged down to Jewell's house and asked her where Robert and I were. She probably didn't know where we were, because we were hiding under the house. After several minutes of frustration, he went back home. I don't know what made me do that, but sometimes boys don't do the right thing.

Before I was old enough to work in the mill, I used to go to aunt Pearl's house and pick up a pint jar of milk for her. She made it like a milkshake. She would put an egg in the milk and sweeten it. It would be cold about nine o'clock because she had left it in her refrigerator. I would take the milk to her every morning, and at the end of the week, she would give me a quarter. That doesn't sound like much, but on Friday, it was enough to get my brother Roger and me into the theater up town. It only cost ten cents a person, so we would buy a nickel bag of popcorn and share it. A nickel bag was a lot in those times.

Aunt Pearl had chickens in the backyard of her house. She kept them fenced in. It was nice to get a few eggs and sometimes a young fryer. You would kill a chicken by holding it by the neck and swinging the chicken round and round, until its head came off. One time, she had a sick chicken she needed to get rid of. She asked me to take it down to the company pasture for her. She was going to give me a quarter to get rid of it. I asked Ray and Roger to go with me. I took a broom handle with me to do the job with. We crossed over the dye ditch and made our way half way to sugar hill. This was where we would get rid of the chicken. I held the chicken by its legs and gave it two or three licks with the broom handle. I dropped the chicken to the ground, where it staggered around for about half a minute, and then it turned toward us and began to chase us. It took several minutes for us to finally beat the chicken to death. I felt sorry for what we had done. We buried the chicken, sang a song, and prayed over it.

The radio was our best entertainment. I remember, every Sunday evening we would gather around the radio and listen to the Jack Benny program. One of my favorite programs was the *Inner Sanctum*. I still remember the creaking door. *Amos and Andy* were also favorites. *Fibber Magee and Molly* were another. Most of Joe Louis's boxing matches were on the radio also. Announcers back then earned their money. I remember the Tony Zale and Rocky Graziano matches all were on the radio. Every Saturday night, there was the grand old opera with Minnie Pearl and Grandpaw Jones. They were my favorites, along with Eddie Arnold.

There were no televisions when we were boys. We had to entertain ourselves with other means. One game we played was "mumbly peg." This was where you took a round stick about six inches long and whittled a taper on the end of it, sort of like a pencil. Then we used a broom handle about thirty-six inches long. We would place the tapered six-inch stick on another short stick, propped up on one end with the tapered part elevated up. We then would take the broom handle and strike the short stick, and it would pop up in the air. Then we would hit the short stick with the broom handle to see who could hit it the furthest.

The girls played jackstones, a game consisting of a small rubber ball about one inch in diameter, and six or eight jackstones made up of metal with legs all over. They would drop the jackstones down on the floor. They would then have to drop the ball and pick up one jackstone and catch the ball, before it bounced again. The next time you dropped the ball and picked up two jackstones, before they hit the floor. The next time three, the next time four, until all the jackstones were picked up. If you missed at any time picking up the jackstones on one bounce of the ball, you would lose your turn. The next player then would have their try at it.

Another thing we boys loved to do was to go to the local Holiness Church where they were having special meetings. If you liked good singing, you would have loved to hear those members sing. They would gather at the front of the church, clap their hands, and glorify God with their singing. As young boys, we did not fully understand all that was going on, but we enjoyed what we were seeing. Sometimes one of them would get happy, begin to talk in tongues, and start running up and down the aisles of the church. They were happy in the Lord. We could stay there for hours at a time. Later in life, after receiving Christ as Saviour, I would understand it better. I was not of the holiness faith. Baptist was my choice of worship, and I have been very happy and blessed in it.

Another place to visit was the black church uptown. Our preacher was invited to their church and accepted the invitation. Their pastor was to preach first. He took his text on the flood.

He began by saying, "Well it rained the first day."

Then the congregation would say, "It rained the first day."

The pastor would then say. "Well it rained the second day," and the congregation would say, "It rained the second day."

He continued through the forty days. After he completed the forty days, one of the sisters told another, "Hold my coat, I'm about to praise the Lord," after which the entire congregation began to praise the Lord. You should have been there.

Halloween was a big time event for us boys in Fullerville. Two or three of us would get together and go through the community making mischief. I never did some of the ugly things that some of the older boys would do, but we were all a nuisance to the community. All toilets were outdoors. Some of the boys would turn over the outhouse of someone who gave them a hard time. To say the least, that was not a nice thing to do. We put a plastic bucket half full of water above the screen door of Jewell's house. None of the screen doors had locks on them. The screen door would be opened enough to place the water bucket, where it would stay above the door. After someone knocked on the door, Jewell came to the door and opened the screen just enough for the bucket of water to fall on her. Needless to say, she was drenched. It seems like we were always picking on Vester Thomas's house. I think that was because we liked him. Most all the houses had the switch box for the main power to the house on the porch. His front porch had a crawl space under it. The switch box was on the corner of the porch. We would slip up to the porch and cut the switch off. We then would jump off the porch and crawl under his front porch. If he had only known we were under there, we would have been in trouble. But he never thought to look under the porch. After he turned the switch back on, he would wait on the porch for a short while and go back into the house. We then would slip out from under the porch and turn his switch off again. We would do this until we tired of it. There was no such thing as trick or treat; that would come a few years later. We thought Halloween was a time for mischief. One of the funniest things I saw was at Cannon Casket Company. The railroad company would bring boxcars there and leave them. The materials needed to build the caskets were shipped in on railcars. There was a boxcar there one day near to where some workers were using a crane for some type of construction. They got the idea to pick up one of the employee's car and place it on top of the boxcar. When the man got off of his shift, he was very surprised to see that his car was not in its usual parking place. He was even more surprised to see his car on top of the boxcar. After a period of laughs all around, they retrieved the car for him.

Plum season was a good time. Plums were abundant everywhere, on the side of the roads and in the fields. There were many varieties of plums. Some were red, some yellow, but all were sweet and good. When the plums were ripe, we would pick them in a gallon bucket and take them home to make homemade wine. We really did not know the proper way to make it, but we tried anyway. We would crush the plums with our fingers and drop them into a churn. We would then cover the churn with a cloth so they could breathe. Sometimes they would ferment and sometimes they didn't do so well. If you really wanted good wine, the Carnes boy's was the place to go. They really knew how to make good wine. Most of the time, we just ate what we picked. We were picking and eating one day up near Hershel Reed's place. I felt something slimy fall around my arm. I looked down as it hit the ground. It was a green snake. It had bitten me on the arm. All it did was form a small knot on my arm like a wasp sting. I was a little afraid but never had any reaction from it.

Easterwood's wash hole was our favorite place to go. The water was always cold. Mr. Easterwood's place was about three-quarters of a mile from our place. Most summer days you could find us making our way up there. The closer we got, the faster we would walk. The last hundred feet or so, we ran. It was a small area where water had pooled up, but we thought it was a fine swimming hole.

We had a lot of fun during dog days. That was a time when snakes were easy to find. We would walk the creek banks going out of the wash hole, and when we found a snake, we would try to kill it. If we couldn't kill it, we ran from it. I really don't know how we made it as boys.

Saturday morning was a time to go to the poolroom. You could play a game of pool for ten cents. Nine-ball was the same price. There was gambling on almost all the tables. If you were playing nine-ball, and you made the nine-ball on the break, it was still ten cents. There were some pretty good players, so you had to be careful whom you played with. I did not consider myself a good player, but I could hold my own with a good number of the guys. My brother, Cecil, was a very good player. Hugh was another very good player. I watched them as they played each other in a nine-ball match. I was worried about Cecil when I saw just how good Hugh was. They were playing for one dollar per game. That might not sound like much by today's standards, but it was a lot back then. They would go back and forth, one winning this game and the other winning the next. After an hour of this, the most either of them would lose would be five or six dollars. The biggest winner was the pool hall.

Another game we played was pill pool. You really did not have to be a great player to play this game, although talent was always an asset. You played by drawing a numbered pill out of a container. The pills were numbered one through fifteen. No one knew which pill the other guy had. The one who would break the balls had no idea which ball belonged to whom. If your ball number should go in on the break, you would be the winner. If no one's ball went in on the break, you would then start making balls by rotation one through fifteen. If the shooter should make your ball number, you would be the winner. Normally, we would play for fifty cents a person. If there were six people in the game, you could make three dollars. The cost of the game to the pool attendant was ten cents on a rotating basis per person. JR was not a very good player, but for some reason, he always wanted to play me a game of nine-ball. He would win every now and then, but I normally could take his money. After a period of time, I would make an excuse to quit because I did not want to take all of his money. We would normally play for fifty cents a game, but after a while, even that was too much. The loser would have to pay the pool hall for that game. Jesse was the pool hall attendant for a good long while. Jesse had lost his hand in a shooting accident. The doctors had placed a device on his right arm that had an attachment that allowed him to pick up objects. He could hold a cue stick with that device, and with it could shoot a good game of pool. He was a little better pool shooter than I was, so I shied away from one-on-one with him, but I would not hesitate to join in on a pill game. There was a lot of loud talking and some cursing, but I never saw any fighting in the poolroom.

I have many memories of my dog, Chipper. He was a shaggy collie dog that had an unusual way of fighting and could hold his own with any dog. I was sitting under the oak tree one day when some neighborhood boys were returning home from rabbit hunting. They had two blue tick hounds with them. They said to me, "You had better watch your dog, or he will get hurt." One of the blue tick dogs ran over to Chipper, and I knew there would be trouble. The blue tick made the mistake of attacking Chipper. Chipper would sit on his rear when fighting. So he sat on his rear and began his attack on the hounds. It didn't take long for Harold to beg me to get Chipper off his dog. Most places I would go, Chipper went with me. I got a paper route with the Atlanta paper. I didn't have any transportation, so I would have to walk to Villa Rica everyday, where they would leave my papers. My route started with eighty papers. I soon built the route up to ninety-five papers. I had a shoulder satchel in which I would place my papers. I would then walk my route from Villa Rica to Fullerville, distributing my papers as

I would go along. Sundays were hard because of the size of the papers. I would most of the time have to take half of the papers, deliver them, and return for the other half. The cost of the paper was twenty-five cents per week. After collecting my money once a week, I would mail the money to the owners of the paper. The amount left over from what I was billed was my profit. Believe me, it was not a lot, because any unpaid amounts from people would be taken from my part. I finally found an old second-hand bicycle that my brother and I shared. It really took a lot of burden off me on my paper route. My dog, Chipper, could not stand to look at a cat, and, if possible, he would kill every one he could catch. My brother delivered the paper one day, and Chipper killed a cat at one of our customer's house. The next day, he delivered the papers again for me. When he arrived at this house, the owner took a gun and shot and killed our dog. That was a sad day for the both of us.

The fondest memories of my youth were centered around baseball. Before I was old enough to play, I would always go to the ball field to watch the games. After all, I had two older brothers on the team. I enjoyed watching Curt and Cecil play their positions. Charlie Bilbo had a small café at the field, and he would give me a little change if I would sell Cokes for him at the game. He would fill a five-gallon bucket with ice and Cokes, and I would go around to the folks at the game and try to sell them. The people who could not get in the grandstand would line up and down the left side of the ballpark and sit on the ground. I will never forget a man to whom I sold a Coke. We would sell the Cokes for a nickel each. I handed him the Coke and offered to open it for him. He said, "I don't need it opened." He then took the Coke, placed the stopper in his mouth, and pulled the stopper off of the bottle with his teeth. My eyes must have been as big as saucers. He looked at me with laughing eyes, as I grimaced in pain as he opened the bottle.

Charlie had a son called Buddy. We were about the same age. He would bring his boxing gloves to the game. He wanted me to box him, and I didn't mind. I loved to box, especially if it was someone about my size. I didn't realize what he was doing at the time, but later when my ankle area began to hurt, I knew what he had been doing. He would jump up on my feet, trying to keep me from being able to move around. It was an unfair tactic, but I was still able to hold my own with him.

Ballgames were so much fun, and a great part of life at Fullerville. I tried out for the mill team when I was seventeen. They needed a catcher, since their regular catcher had decided to stop playing. I loved to catch and was pretty good at it, so I made first-string catcher my first year out. When springtime came around, we would go to the field and practice every day on pitching, catching, and batting. On baseball game day, when we were playing in Fullerville, I would make my way early in the morning to the ball field. A couple of the guys would go as well. Our mission was to chop up any grass that may have sprung up on the infield. After the sprigs of grass were removed, someone with a tractor would drag the infield. This was done with a heavy screen attached to the tractor. After the infield had been dragged to satisfaction, it was time to mark the lines down the left and right fields and the coach's box at third and first base. After this, we would mark the batter's box. We had a device on wheels, which would hold the lime that makes the mark on the field. We would fill the device with lime, and as we pushed it along the foul lines, it would dispense a small stream of lime on the ground. All this was hard work and would take a large portion of the morning. After we prepared the field, we would return home and put on our baseball uniforms. We would then return to the field for batting and fielding practice before the game. We would spend the great portion of the day with these activities. By late evening, you were a very tired boy, but it was a good tired, because you were doing something you really enjoyed.

Pete lived close to me, and we would walk to the field together. To say I was excited would be putting it mildly. Pete was an outfielder. His greatest asset was his speed. He could run like the wind. If he had just known his speed was such a great asset, he could have bunted three hundred. He would, in a few years, go on to play minor league ball. Fred was another of our outfielders. He had lost some fingers on one of his hands, but it did not hinder him from throwing a ball. Fred's strength was his ability to hit the ball, and you could depend on him for a base hit when one was needed. Fred too would go on, at a later date, to play minor league ball. Hayne Waldrop was our manager. He had some superstitions, but he was a good manager. When he was coaching third base, he would put a glove in the upper-right-hand corner of the coaching box. Also, when we went to an away game, I had to ride in the back seat of his car on the driver's side. No one was to have that seat but me. There were three Sauls on that team my first year. My brother Curt was on first base, my brother Cecil on shortstop, and myself as catcher. Cecil was a smooth fielding shortstop. If a ball was anywhere near him, it was a caught ball. My brother Curt was a good hitter. I have seen him rattle the house that stood just beyond left field. I'll never forget the first time I came to bat in a game with my uniform on. I was so nervous, I could not keep my left foot from jumping up and down. Needless to say, I struck out. It takes a while for a young man to learn to hit, especially if there is no one to give him advice. Thankfully, my hitting would soon come around. I had great confidence in my catching ability. I never saw a pitcher that I could not catch. After a couple of years, I was offered a job with the Carrollton Hornets. They were a team from Carrollton that was in the Georgia Alabama league. Curt did not want me to go. He said that they just wanted me to catch batting practice and that I would just get my fingers broken up. I have always regretted not going for the tryout.

All the small towns had a baseball team. We played a pretty fast brand of baseball. I remember very well the first nighttime baseball game I caught. It was in Clarksdale. They always had a good team. Lefty Temple was our pitcher for that night. He was getting on in years for a ballplayer, and his velocity was not very good. Temple had a knuckle ball that you could count the stitches on the ball as it came at you. The ball floated around, and it was hard for a young catcher to get a handle on it. I caught about half his pitches in my breastplate. If the other team started to get to him, Hayne would put J. E. Waldrop in behind him. He had a hard fastball, and to catch him, I had to put a cloth for padding inside my mitt. After hitting against the slow pitch of Lefty Temple, it was quiet a contrast to hit at a ninety-plus-mile-an-hour fastball.

The equipment in my day was far inferior to the equipment supplied today. The old iron masks we wore were heavy, and when a tipped ball caught you in the mask just right, it was like being hit in the face with a boxing glove. The breastplates were also heavy, with a long tail to help protect your crouch. By the time you got all that, plus your shin-guards, on, you felt like a warrior going to battle with an armored suit on. Those old pocket mitts made a nice popping sound, but they were hard on the palm of your hand. Now the mitts are designed to catch the ball in the web, which offers a much more comfortable position, but I loved it. You feel like somebody when you can see if the other players are in the proper positions. Once you learn what a pitcher can do, you can call the game to suit his best talent. We were in the West Georgia League the first year I was on the team. Our strongest competitor was Newnan. We won twenty-two straight ballgames that year and played Newnan for the league championship. We were fortunate enough to win that game and bring the trophy home with us.

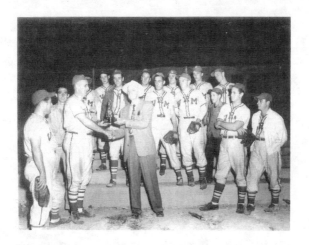

Dimmer Lee was one of our pitchers. He was a good pitcher. We were playing a game at Clarksdale and Dimmer was our pitcher that night. Sometimes you would see really good players come into our league. Clarksdale had a player named Greengrass who actually belonged to the Yankees farm chain. He could hit a ball a mile with little effort. When he came to bat, the guys shouted to Dimmer, "Throw him your spider ball." Dimmer pumped once and threw the ball. The last time we saw that ball, it was going over the right field fence and gaining speed. Dimmer took a lot of kidding about his spider ball.

Another fun game was in our home park. Lefty Temple was pitching. He was a tall lanky guy and depended on his stuff to get people out. He had one pitch where he would fall off the mound toward first base, and with an underhand motion that almost touched the ground, he would deliver his pitch. Socco Stockwell was playing first base for the opposing team. Socco at one time played some for the Atlanta Crackers. It was his turn to bat. He was a left-handed hitter, and when Hershel came at him with that fall away curve ball, Socco jumped back and the umpire shouted, "Strike." Socco looked at the umpire and said, "What was that?" The umpire said, "I said it was a strike." Socco said, "I know darn well it was a strike, but I want to know what it was." We had a lot of fun games, but they were all serious in our eyes.

Everyone in our mill village received their mail in a community mailbox. The mailbox was rather large and located on the front street about center way between the switch track and the ballpark. There was no other mailbox, and so if you received mail, you would get it in that box. I never knew of anyone complaining about mail being stolen. Most people in the village respected other people's property. I suppose since all mail was in the same box, you could not help but know who sent mail to one another. During World War II, mail received from our soldiers came in an envelope with red and blue on the edges. We had a good number of our village boys in the service of our country. I had two brothers serving in the World War II and one brother who served after the war was over. I was never asked to serve at any time. My age was perfect for the Korean War, but by the time they were drafting for that war my first child had been born, and I was reclassified. I never received any notice from the draft board after that. It was a great day in our community when the announcement came on the radio that Japan had surrendered. It would not be too much longer until our boys would be coming home. It would be such a wonderful thing if the nations of the world could live together in peace.

Everyone in the mill village knew one another. There were nicknames for almost everyone. There was Surpy, Barehead, Bum, Lightening, Hoot, Rusty, Shug, Peewee, Budoak, Slick, and many others. During those days of depression, we had folks to come by the house, who were hungry and looking for work. We never turned one away but always managed to find something for them to eat.

There was no inside plumbing, but every house had an outhouse. They had hired a man to clean the outhouses once a month. He had a mule and a wagon on which there were fifty-five gallon drums. He would shovel the waste from the outhouses into the drums. He then would sprinkle some type of sanitizer under the outhouse. In order to do this, most of the time he had a supply of whiskey with him. Once our policeman decided he was drunk and decided to lock him up, upon which he quit his job as sanitary man. It didn't take the city long to apologize to him and assure him he could have his whiskey.

Most men smoked Prince Albert tobacco and OCB leaves to roll their own. Not many could afford ready-roll cigarettes. Times were hard during the depression. They sometimes would throw half smoked cigarettes away, and the young boys would pick them up. Sometimes they would find a tobacco can that had been thrown away. They would break open the discarded cigarettes and pour the remaining tobacco into the tobacco can. Pretty soon, they would have a half to full can of unused tobacco. They could buy a book of OCB leaves for a nickel, and they were in business. It was not the advisable thing to do, but times were hard back then.

Flour was sold in twenty-five pound sacks. Biscuits were cooked just about every meal. The sacks were made of a nice print cloth, which the ladies could use to make a print dress. Some of those dresses looked nice, and the ladies were not ashamed to wear them. Just about everybody bought groceries at the country grocery store. They would charge what you bought, and every payday, you would go and pay your bill. When Edith and I first married, I carried on that tradition. The first week of our marriage, I went to pay my bill. The store owner said, "That will be five dollars. What are you trying to do, starve that girl to death?" What he didn't know was that we ate most of our meals that first week at Edith's mother's. So when he made his comment, I said, "You know how much my bill is this week, don't you? He said, "Yes." I said, "I promise you won't know how much it is next week." I never bought another grocery from that store. I paid cash from that day on.

In Fullerville, all streets and sidewalks were unpaved. The main road through Fullerville was Highway 101. It was also an unpaved road. The first waterline we had was installed by the WPA. The WPA was set up by President Roosevelt in the thirties to give men an opportunity to work and to make a little money. Although the WPA never served more than a quarter of the nations unemployed, it was unprecedented in its scale. It was so popular with the people that it contributed greatly to Franklin D. Roosevelt's electoral victory in 1936. There were not many job opportunities during that period of time. I'll never forget how those men were lined up on the road about ten feet apart. Each one of them had a pick and shovel. They would dig the ditch, and others would come behind them and install the water pipe. This was the first time any of those mill houses would have inside water. Prior to this, water had to be carried into the homes from a community well that everyone shared.

Another job opportunity for men was the CCC. This was also set up by our president to further provide jobs for the unemployed. As boys, we called them cover county convicts. They stayed in barracks like army boys and were provided clothes and other essentials necessary for good hygiene. They would leave the barracks in the morning loaded on trucks. They would proceed to wherever they were assigned to work that day. The Twin Lakes in Villa Rica was built by the CCC. They cut timber and cleaned areas necessary for the project. Several of us boys would make the long walk over there just to watch them work.

One time the county allowed prisoners to work at different places around town. One day they were working at the school. During lunch break, I saw one of the convicts sitting under a shade tree. I walked over to where he was and spoke to him. I was about to eat, and he looked so pitiful, I offered him my sandwich. He gladly accepted it, and with about three bites, he had eaten all of it. For some reason, I was not afraid of him, but I kept at a respectable distance.

If you wanted to take a shower, you would have to go

to Grubbs Barber Shop. He had installed a shower in the back of his shop, and for a quarter, you could take a shower there. Rayford was a good barber, and his shop always stayed busy. My first daughter, Dianne, got her first hair trim at Rayford's Barber Shop. Rayford's house was only about fifty yards from his shop. He had a squirrel he kept as a pet. That squirrel got out one day and climbed the tree in front of his house. He asked me to climb up there and get his pet. I climbed up to the limb the squirrel was on, the squirrel looked at me, and I looked at him.

Rayford said, "Get him, Hoot."

I said, "I am afraid he might bite me."

He said, "No it won't."

I reached for the squirrel, and he nailed me between my thumb and my forefinger. I threw the squirrel to the ground, and Rayford laughed and laughed. I didn't think it was very funny. After all, it was my finger that was bitten.

The older men kept us boys concerned when we were out at night. They told the story of the "great white thang." It was a common practice to sit around after dark and tell scary stories. When we would finally go home, we would run all the way. Pete had to go to Bills store at dusty dark one evening. He left the store with something in a brown paper sack. There was a small wooden bridge between the dirt road and the sidewalk near his house. We were sitting on our front porch that was across the street from Bill's store. The small bridge was in front of our house. As Pete left the store and was about halfway across the road, someone yelled, "Watch out for the thang." Pete was very fast on his feet. He broke out in a run and attempted to cross the little bridge. He tripped on the bridge and turned a flip up into the air. The sack he was carrying was tossed up into the air. Pete landed on his feet and caught the sack before it hit the ground. He was gone in a flash back toward his house. We all laughed.

Roger, Ray, and I were just boys at the time when we got together and decided we were going to open our own grocery store. In order to be a partner in the store, you had to steal something from Bill's grocery store and bring it back to our hideout. We were then going to sell those things in our grocery store. We agreed that Mama would trade with us and maybe Ray's mother would also. Roger stole a potato, and Ray stole an onion. It was my time to take something. I went out to Bills store and paid for a small cake. The cakes were all mixed together on a table, and I was told to pick one out that I liked. Mrs. Florence and a friend were sitting about middle-way down in the store and talking to one another. I stood over that table a long time pretending to be picking out what I wanted. I was taking such a long time that Mrs. Florence and her friend both knew I was up to something. At that time, I did not know that they suspected anything. I was afraid, but I went ahead, put one small cake in my pocket, and took the other one in my hand. The one in my pocket was to be my contribution to our new grocery store, which now included a potato, an onion, and a small cake. Mrs. Florence did not say anything to me at the time, although they had caught me red handed. I loved Bill and Imma Florence, because since the death of my father they had been my mentors. Mrs. Florence reported this incident to my mama. Needless to say, I felt awful. My mama made me go to Bill's store and apologize to them for what I had done. This was the most embarrassing thing I had ever done in my life. As I stood there before Bill in his store and asked his forgiveness, I could only drop my head. Bill was hurt as well, because of what had happened. He talked to me for some time about how I should not do such a thing. I think he was just as hurt as I was. I shall never forget this as long as God lets me live. I have never again in my lifetime had any desire to take anything that does not belong to me.

In the summer months and on into harvest time, I would work some for Ray Tyson. Ray owned a farm off of Highway 78. He would pick me up and bring me home. Freddy Mae would always fix our dinner, and I looked forward to her meals. Sometimes, we picked cotton all day, and at other times, we would gather hay and put it into his barn. All these things were hard work, and at evening time, you were very tired. One day we were working in the field across the other side of Highway 78. Ray decided we had left an important tool at the house, and wanted me to ride the horse back to the house and get it. I said okay, and he lifted me up on the horse's back. The minute he did, the horse took off like he had been shot out of a gun. He headed back toward the highway, and I was hoping that no cars were coming. Luckily, none were, and he made it across the highway. When the horse reached the top of a small hill, I bailed off but held the reigns in my hand. I walked all the way back to Ray's house leading the horse by his reigns. I retrieved the tool we were missing and led the horse all the way back. I was afraid to ride the horse. I didn't know if I could control him or not, and I still had the highway on my mind.

You haven't lived until you have stood on top of a wagonload of hay, used a pitchfork to throw the loose hay into a window at the top of the barn, and then moved the hay deeper into the barn so you could get more hay in. No one had to rock you to sleep at night. Not much money was involved, but what I got I appreciated, because that was the only way I had of getting any. Money was hard to come by in those days.

I had finished two years of high school. I was fifteen years of age and nearing my sixteenth birthday, which was on the Fourth of July. You were only required to go through the eleventh grade in order to graduate back at that time. I needed two more years to graduate from school. We were living in the house with my brother, Curtis, and his wife, Esma, and their three children, Richard, John Wayne, and Linda. There was my mother, my younger brother, Roger, and myself. We had three bedrooms, a kitchen, and an outhouse. One morning, I shall never forget, I was called into the kitchen with my mother and my brother, Curtis. I will never forget the news I was about to get if I live to be a hundred. I was told that a job had been obtained for me at the cotton mill after I turned sixteen, and they had given me a mill house. I would have to take my mother, my brother, Roger, and myself to live there. I would not be able to continue going to school and graduate. Looking back now, I can see where they were trying to solve a problem of too many in one house. As I was told how it would be and that I would not be able to continue in school, I felt as if a knife had been stabbed into my heart. I did not cry while in their presence, but after leaving the room and making my way down a path between our house and the next mill house, my heart was breaking and I have never had such a letdown feeling in my life. I could not keep the tears back, but I didn't let any of them see me crying. After my sixteenth birthday, I went to Carrollton, picked up my birth certificate, gave it to the mill office, and started my job in the mill. We moved into a four-room mill house. My rent was twenty-five cents a room per week. I was making sixty-two cents an hour. My mother was not working at the time, and each payday, I would take five dollars for myself and give her the rest of my check. That was all right because things were not so high back then. I could play a game of pool for ten cents a game.

One employee of the mill always had money in his pocket. He sold a little whiskey on the side. He would take advantage of some of the guys there who always seemed to not be able to make it until payday. Payday at the mill was on a Friday. He would buy their check during the week for ten dollars less than it was worth. At payday, they would sign the check and give it to him. You would think they would wise up and stop this practice, but I guess they were too dumb to learn.

Saturday morning, some of the older men would go down the switch track toward the lumber mill. Where the rails ended, there was an old wood road going farther into the woods where a crap game was started. There was plenty of bootleg liquor on hand, and sometimes, it got a little rowdy. I would go sometime just to watch the show. Most of the time, it was just a lot of loud talk and no fighting. Jack showed me how to hide a half pint liquor bottle so that, if the police were to pat you down, they most likely would overlook it. You would place it under your belt at the small of your back, and when you were patted down, it was hard to detect.

About one hundred feet outside the cotton mill door, there was a huge oak tree. There was a bench built in a circle around the oak tree. When the doffers would catch up with their work, they would go outside and sit on the wide bench, until the foreman would whistle. Then the men would go into the mill again to remove the full bobbins and replace them with empty ones. Many stories were told under that old tree, some true and some not so true. There was quite an argument at times about who was the fastest doffer. If that old tree could talk, you would have heard some wild tales. My job was doffer in the twister room. My working buddies were Landrum, Lewis, and Roy. Roy was about my age, but Landrum and Lewis were older than I was. I loved to hear Roy talk about his thirty-two Ford. He couldn't pronounce *thirty* properly. Roy called it *thuty*-two. Every time we would go out to the old tree, I would ask him what model the truck was. He would say "thuty-two." He never realized I was making fun.

Roy and I were doffing partners. One day, there was quite a bit of tension between us. We were doffing a machine, he was on one side, and I was on the other side. We were racing to see who could finish his side first. The tension continued to build. As we both seemed to finish together, we decided to end it with a fistfight. We lunged at one another and began swinging our fists. Suddenly, something grabbed me from behind. Commer, who was our foreman, had grabbed me by my overall straps and jerked me away. Commer was a big man, but as a rule, a gentle man. He made Roy and I shake hands, and that was the end of our fight.

Sometimes, between doffing rounds, we would go to Preacher's store and buy an R.C. Cola and a pack of white peanuts. We would take a few drinks from the R.C. bottle and pour some of the peanuts into the bottle. We thought this was a nice little treat, and it was pretty good. About mid-morning, Preacher would take orders to be delivered from his café. Oree always had to have an egg sandwich with mustard. Preacher sold a lot of hamburgers and did pretty well for himself with his café business.

There was always excitement around the cement jail. If folks got too drunk, they would wind up in the jail. There were bars at the only window. The jail was divided into two rooms, which were separated by floor to ceiling bars. Normally, the entrance door was open, so you could walk in through the first room to the main lock-up room. All through the day and into the night, you could hear the prisoners yelling and taking on. It was disturbing to anyone who lived close to the jail. Casey was locked up for being drunk. He had a drinking habit and could not control it. Super was a good friend of Casey's and stopped by to see him.

Casey said, "Shoot, Super get me out of here."

Super said, "I can't because you are drunk."

Super got a big laugh out of that. Normally, an overnight stay was enough, just so they could sober up.

Villa Rica has always been blest with good doctors. There was B. C. Powell, Ernest Powell, Ernest Jr. Powell, Dr. Berry, and Dr. Hogue. Dr. B. C. Powell was the elder of the Powell's. Dr. B. C. had his own way of driving a car. He would start off in low gear and most times would just leave it there. On one occasion, he was driving, and Dr. Earnest was riding with him.

After a few miles down the road, Dr. Earnest said, "Do you know you still have the car in first gear?"

Dr. B. C. looked at him and said, "I ought to, I put it there."

There were very few automatic transmissions in those days. Dr. Earnest Powell was our family doctor when I was at home with Mama. Back in the thirties, a doctor would make house calls. Those days are gone forever. I can still see him, as he would get out of his car, carrying his black bag with him. He always had his faithful nurse, Dura, with him. I don't think he could have functioned without her. Mama's children were born in her home. He would give a few pills, or maybe a shot if needed, and he would be on his way. Edith and I were required to have a blood test before we were married. Dr. Hogue was the one we went to for the test. He didn't have any problem finding the vein in my arm, and I was through in just a minute. But Edith had smaller veins, and Dr. Hogue had a very hard time finding hers. He was getting on in years, which only added on to the problem. I thought he would never hit the vein. He just kept sticking and sticking, and I felt like telling him to stop. He finally found the vein, and I was so relieved. After Edith and I married, we chose Dr. Earnest, junior, as our family doctor. Edith and I both were really pleased with him. I thought he was the best doctor there was anywhere. He assisted my wife in the birth of all our girls. His office was in the Powell-Berry-Powell Clinic, which was built to serve the people's medical needs. That building is listed as a historical site today.

Every year or so, the health department would set up in the cotton mill for the purpose of giving free shots to all the village people. I received my smallpox vaccination at the cotton mill. Other shots were given for prevention of typhoid, whooping cough, and diphtheria.

Fullerville was annexed into the city of Villa Rica in 1956. A year or so before that, there was an election held at Fullerville in the little one room courthouse to let the people decide if they wanted to become annexed into the city of Villa Rica. On election day, after the votes were counted, it was discovered that there were one hundred votes cast. There were ninety-nine votes that said no and only one vote that said yes. Well, you might know, it was told who cast the yes vote. The guys at the mill made a big deal out of this. My brother, Cecil, and one or two other guys got together around the old tree at the mill. The one that voted yes worked on the same job that I was doing in the mill. So I was able to see his reaction to what they did next. They made a mock grave next to the bench we sat on between doffing rounds. A cross was placed at one end of the grave, which bore the inscription, *"The Lone Vote."* At the other end of the grave, which consisted of dirt piled up, there was an old pair of brogan shoes stuck into the dirt. An old hat was placed on the cross. All this was done while the lone voter was inside the mill and out of sight. We finished our doffing round on the twister frames and proceeded out to the oak tree for a rest and a smoke. When we got there, the grave was staring us in the face. We sat down on the bench in silence.

He looked at me after a few minutes and said, "You had something to do with that, didn't you?"

I assured him that I did not. After a few more minutes, he jumped off the bench and began kicking at the mock grave. It did not take long to flatten it out. Needless to say, he was the subject of many jokes in the future.

As a boy, I walked to school by way of the switch tracks, which went from Fullerville to the mainline and then a hundred or so yards to where I left the tracks to go on the school. From there, it was only a hundred yards to the school grounds. Many days, as I made my way up those switch tracks, I would look out across the open fields adjacent to the tracks and think to myself, if I only had a gun I could go rabbit hunting out there anytime I wanted to. I did not own a gun, and neither did my older brother, who I was living with at the time. God hears the wishes of our heart and sometimes supplies them.

One summer, while school was out, I spent a week in Atlanta with my uncle, Little Bud, whose real name was Loy Elzie Sauls, and my Aunt Lois. They had two daughters, Ann and Lucille. On the day I was to go back home, my uncle showed me a single shot twenty-two rifle. He asked me if I would like to have it, and of course,

I was so excited and said, "Yes, I would." I thought this was the greatest gift anyone could have. He carried me to the Greyhound Bus Station and put me on my way back home to Villa Rica and on to Fullerville. I carried the rifle in my hands, which was something you would not be allowed to do today. I got off the bus in Villa Rica and walked to Fullerville clutching the rifle in my hands all the way. I would use that rifle many times, as I would go to the woods and "still hunt" for squirrels. To "still hunt" you would find a place where you knew where squirrels frequented. You would sit really still, until you could hear the squirrel moving in the trees. Once you spotted him, you would shoot. Sometimes you would hit, and sometimes you would miss; but always, it was a lot of pleasure. I used that rifle for a few years, until I was able to purchase a double-barreled shotgun for myself. I then passed the rifle on to my nephew, John. I think he was as pleased to get it as I was when it was given to me by my uncle.

Hunting was a fun thing to do. If you wanted to go rabbit hunting, it was no trouble to round up some dogs to take with you. Most dogs were not penned up but roamed freely in the neighborhood. All you had to do was whistle a few times, and when the dogs saw your gun, they were ready to go. Ollie, Roy, and I were hunting together one day. I had a Fox double-barreled, sixteen-gauge that Edith had bought me for Christmas. I was not a very good shot with the gun, but Roy was even worse. Ollie could shoot the gun pretty well. The dogs jumped a rabbit and were carrying it down a brush and tree-lined ditch. The dogs were barking louder and louder. I heard a shot.

Roy immediately yelled out, "Run, dang you with your head shot off."

He had not touched the rabbit. We would laugh about that for many days to come.

Glen had one of the best possum dogs you could find anywhere. He called him League. Glen loved to possum hunt. He asked me to go with him one night. I said okay, and we were on our way. We carried carbide lights to see our way through the woods. Glen had a flashlight, and I carried the carbide light. We had gone to the woods located off the Dallas Highway over toward Twin Lakes and the old sulfur mines. League, our dog, was having one of his best nights ever. As soon as he would tree one possum, he would tree another. We put the possums in a burlap sack we carried with us. After we had gotten three possums into the sack, Glen said that was enough. I'll never forget that walk back down Dallas Highway with the burlap sack full of possums. I carried them, holding the sack in my right hand, and thrown across my back. Every now and then, those possums would start to crawl in the sack. If you have never experienced possums crawling up your back, you haven't lived. Luckily, you could slap them while in the sack, and they would "sull." So you would have a little peace after the possums "sulled." Glen had some wire boxes he had made, and that is where he would keep the possums. He would dry feed them for a couple of weeks, before they would be ready to eat. Possums will eat anything in the wild, so the cleansing process was necessary. I only remember one occasion when Mama fixed possum for dinner. I didn't care for the possum, but the sweet potatoes she lined around the possum were delicious.

Eugene was Glen's son. He and I played together as young boys. Glen decided to go squirrel hunting up to Barn's Woods. He wanted Eugene and me to go with him. He had decided we were going to hunt until dark and spend the night in the woods. Glen could not hear very well, but he had an exceptional way of spotting a squirrel in a tree. He would say, "Listen for them and show me where you heard the sound." I pointed to a tree where I heard sounds, and Glen looked for a minute. I didn't see anything, but Glen raised his gun and fired. A squirrel came falling out of the tree. I was amazed that he could see that well. When it was too dark to see, we found a clearing in the woods and built a campfire. We sat around and talked for a while, and then I lay down on the ground and went to sleep. I must have been there for some time by myself. When I awoke, I noticed that neither Eugene nor Glen were there. I didn't know what to think, when suddenly I heard Eugene and Glen coming back to the campsite. They had gone to get some water in a pot. Glen boiled us some squirrels in that pot over the campfire. To a very hungry boy that night, I thought it was the best meat I had ever eaten. We got up early the next morning, and we killed a few more squirrels and headed for home.

Henry Carter and Mr. Brooks were men who lived in two of the mill houses. These houses were located near to the boiler room side of the mill. They had easy access to the mill from where they lived. Both of them were fine gentlemen, as well as were their families. I felt right at home with them when I visited their home. Morris was Mr. Brook's son. We played together a lot in the company pasture behind the mill. There was a pinto horse in that pasture, and if it ever saw me, it would chase me to the fence. I don't know if he would have done me any harm, but he knew I was afraid of him.

Mr. Brooks was in charge of the boilers, and Henry was his assistant. Maintenance had to be done, and the boilers had to be kept fired with coal. Coal was delivered by rail. The cars were stopped on a bridge just above the boiler room. It was situated so that as coal was released from the rail car, it would pile up near to the boiler room and would then be shoveled into a wheelbarrow. It was then carried up a gang-walk to the mouth of the boiler where it was placed into the boilers. These two men did a fine job of keeping the boilers so that steam could drive the main wheel and keep the mill running. There was a problem with the boiler one day. It was in danger of blowing up. Everyone had moved out of the area. With a bold move, Henry ran back into the boiler room, turned a few valves, and calmed the boiler down.

Some of the guys said, "Henry, were you not afraid to go back in there?"

Henry said, "Well, my common sense told me not to, but my liquor told me to do it."

Henry loved his whisky and always seemed to have some around. One day, Henry was going possum hunting with some of the white boys in the village. Everybody liked Henry, and he was welcome to go hunting anytime he wanted to go. Henry said, "Boys, every time the dogs tree a possum, we are going to take a drink." Time went along, and the dogs had not treed a possum. Henry said, "Boys, it looks like we are going to have to slip one on the dogs." It wasn't very long till Henry was feeling pretty good. He fell into a deep hole in the dark and had to be helped out. Every time I think of Henry, I think about slipping one on the dogs.

When I was a young boy, I would ask Henry if I could borrow his shotgun to hunt awhile. He never refused to let me use his gun. It was a twelve-gauge, double-barrel shotgun. It had hammers on it, which had to be pulled back before you could fire it. I would go to Bill's grocery store and buy six shotgun shells. That was all I could afford at the time. You learned not to go about shooting at empty squirrel's nests. If you did, you would run out of shells pretty quick. I always would thank him for the use of his gun. Henry's wife's name was Nell. Nell would help Mama at times with her ironing. If Henry was not at home when I wanted to borrow his gun, Nell would let me have it. They liked me, and I liked them.

Anyone who wanted to have a hog was able to do so. People in the village who wanted to raise a hog could put one there. We had a hog and it was my duty to feed him at evening time. We would mix shorts with water into large buckets and take it to the hog pen. I loved to watch the hogs eat. Another thing they would eat was coal. We would throw some coal into the lot just to hear them crunch it up. When the weather turned really cold, it was hog-killing time. At hog-killing time, you could take your hog to the mill. They provided A-frames to hang the hogs on for cleaning. They also furnished all the hot water you needed to help with cleaning. I loved hog-killing time. We would pitch in with our neighbors and help each other during that time. Although I was young, I was given a knife and shown how to cut up the meat. Some folks just cut the whole thing up in sausage. Others would save the tenderloin, shoulders, and hams. They would put the meat in boxes and salt it down. This was to preserve the meat. Folks shared with one another in our village. The mill provided some fencing for the people. Everyone would share their meat with their neighbor. We were as a family and all shared with one another.

The young men were always pulling pranks on one another. One evening Mack, Rob, Lee Roy, and John were riding around in Lee Roy's car. Lee Roy always carried his shotgun in the trunk of his car. Mack, Rob, and Lee Roy had plotted together to pull a trick on John. They had decided to stop at Hershell's watermelon patch. They had pumped John full of how mean Hershell was. They said if he were to catch you in his watermelon patch, he would shoot you. Regardless of all the warnings they had, all three made their way into the watermelon patch. What John did not know was that Lee Roy had slipped his shotgun out of the trunk of the car. It was a dark night, and one could easily hide from the others. They had made their way to about the middle of the patch when Mack shouted, "Look out, here comes Hershell." About that time, Lee Roy fired his shotgun into the air and shouted, "Run for it." Rob hid himself in the field, and Lee Roy, Mack, and John ran for the car. They jumped into the car, and Lee Roy cranked the car. John said, "Wait, Rob is not here yet." Mack said, "He's been shot." Lee Roy sped away without him. They drove about for some ten minutes, and of course, John was in a panic. They finally drove back to the scene and found Rob standing on the side of the road waiting for them. What a cruel joke to play on John, but that's the way that group acted.

When the cotton mill went on hard times, I took a job with Cannon Casket Company. My brother, Cecil, was one of the supervisors, and he helped me to get a job. I was put in the shipping and receiving department. Our duties were to load caskets onto flat trailers for shipment to Atlanta. One day, one of the drivers came in barking orders. He wanted his trailer loaded out now! He continued to bark out at us on the loading dock. I finally got tired of his barking out orders and told him, if he wanted it loaded out any quicker, he could grab a hand truck for himself. He then said, "I'll just go to the office and see about that." I told him that if he expected to get to Atlanta today, he had better find him a place to sit down and leave us alone. He finally drifted back out of sight, and we loaded him just as we would have any other driver.

One Friday the thirteenth, we were loading empty casket boxes for shipment to Atlanta. I would go inside and run my hand trucks under an empty box and take it to the dock for loading. I repeated this process over and over. On one of my trips inside, I saw this box sitting there and kind of leaning to the left. I assumed I had found another empty box. I ran my hand trucks under the box and made a pull toward me. What I did not realize was that there was six hundred pounds of

EDMUND "HOOT" SAULS

hardware in that box. It started at me and would not stop. I fell to the floor, and the box landed propped up on top of some caskets, which were laying there on the floor. There was just enough room under that heavy box to keep it off me. I crawled out from under the box and thanked God for protecting me. About an hour later, I became sick and had to take the rest of the day off. My nerves were still on edge.

There was a black guy who worked there. He was a good guy, and we clowned with one another a lot. He was a very strong man. I was pretty strong myself in my younger years. We got to wrestling around one day. I tried to throw him, and he tried to throw me. We wound up on the ground, and I knew I had more than I could handle. His arms were around my head, and I thought I would never get out of his hold on me. Somehow I managed to get loose, and we were both glad of it I think. I avoided any future wrestling matches with him. I finally got off the loading dock, and they put me in charge of boxing up the wooden caskets for shipment. We had one man who worked in the metal department who was quite a man himself. He could pick up one end of a metal sealer casket and head it up by himself. He clowned around a lot and loved to drink moonshine liquor. One day, he laid down in one of the caskets. I never would have done such a thing, but he did. I am too superstitious for that. A year or so later, he was in the back seat of a taxi and chugalugged a pint jar of white liquor, passed out, and died. I don't think lying down in the casket had anything to do with it, but I wouldn't guarantee it.

Some years later a good friend of mine, Charles Turner,

would help me get a job with the electrical company he was working with. I got in just in time, because about a year later, a high school diploma was required, along with two years of algebra. Since I had made it in before those requirements were necessary, I was able to keep my job.

Edith and I were renting a house that was owned by her aunt, Ruth Crews. The house was located in Fullerville. This was where we were living when I got my job with Brooks Allison Company. Brooks Allison Company was located in Atlanta, Georgia. Their office was located on Edgewood Avenue right across from the city auditorium. My friend, Turner, drove his car back and forth to Atlanta each day to work. He had several people who rode with him to their work places. There was not enough room for me to ride with him at that time. Several months later, a place would be come available for me to ride in his car, but in the meantime, I had to provide my own way. I didn't trust my car to get me to Atlanta, so I rode the bus to work until the opening would come available in Turner's car. Southeastern Motor Lines ran a bus line from Carrollton to Atlanta. They came through Villa Rica, and that is where I would catch the bus. I walked from our home in Fullerville to the bus station, which was a distance of about two miles. The Southeastern Motor Line bus destination was the Greyhound Bus Station in Atlanta. After arriving at the Greyhound Bus Station, I then would walk to Edgewood Avenue, where I would meet the electrician I would work with for that day. After a days work, I would walk from Brooks Allison's office back to the bus station. Then I would catch the bus back to Villa Rica, where I would walk the two miles back to my home. Needless to say, I was happy when a place came open in Turner's car.

The apprentice wiremen were obligated to attend apprentice school. So on the nights I had to go to school, I had to walk from Brooks Allison's office to Smith Hughes Vocational School. It was a distance of about a half mile. After class was finished, I would then walk from school to the Greyhound bus station. I would catch the bus to Villa Rica and then walk the two miles to my home.

The walk from school to the bus station was quite interesting at times. I had people stop me on numerous occasions wanting a handout. They would always have an excuse for needing something that usually resulted in asking for money. One evening as I arrived at the bus station, I was stopped by a man who wanted a dollar to help him with his bus fare home. I could tell by his looks he had been drinking. I guess I must have felt sorry for him, because I gave him the dollar. I boarded my bus for home and leaned back in the seat. The bus had not gone two miles when the scripture from the Bible hit me. It was Ezekiel 3:18 (KJV) that says,

> When I say unto the wicked, thou shall surely die; and thou givest him not warning, nor speakest to warn the wicked from his wicked way, to save his life; the same wicked man shall die in his iniquity; but his blood will I require at thine hand.

I prayed and asked God to forgive me for not presenting God's plan of salvation to him.

After my first year of apprentice training, I was to be voted into the Local Union 613. The meeting was in the evening hours. I made my way to the union hall and waited there until time for the meeting to start. The meeting lasted for some time, and it was late when it was over. I met a young man there who I knew from apprentice school, and he said he would give me a ride as far as Douglasville. I said okay, and thought I could catch the bus to Villa Rica. We arrived in Douglasville a little too late to catch my bus. He let me out of his car in the middle of the main street in Douglasville. It looked like the most deserted place I had ever seen. I began to try to hitch a ride. Finally a tractor/trailer came by and stopped for me. I thought to myself, I've got it made now. I sat down in that big rig, we exchanged greetings, and we were on our way to Villa Rica, I thought. About five miles west of Douglasville on Highway 78, there was a truck stop. The truck driver said he needed a cup of coffee. I thought to myself that a cup of coffee might not be too bad. He pulled his big truck into the parking lot, and instead of getting out of the truck to get his coffee, he leaned back and went sound to sleep. I'm looking at him in disbelief and was uncertain what to do. I knew that he possibly could sleep there until morning. I opened the door and climbed to the ground. I entered the truck stop café and ordered a cup of coffee. There was another truck driver there drinking a cup of coffee, and I asked him if he would let me ride with him to Villa Rica. He said that he could not because his insurance would not allow it. We sat there for some time, and I guess he must have felt sorry for me, because he looked over at me and said, "Come on, and I will give you a ride to Villa Rica." We arrived in Villa Rica sometime around midnight. I never was never so glad to get out of that truck. I walked the two miles home and was happy to get there.

When I was hired into Brooks Allison Company, my pay scale was one dollar and twenty-five cents an hour. I never made over two dollars an hour during my entire apprenticing years. After taking the test for journeyman wireman and successfully passing it, I was upgraded to three dollars an hour. I thought I had become a rich man.

I owe a lot to my friend and to all who helped me with my training. Most of all, I thank God for making a way for me to have this opportunity and giving me the strength to finish course.

In 1957, I was an apprentice wireman working for Brooks Allison Company. Leonard Honea, who would later become our shop superintendent, and I were sent to Dobbins Air Base in Marietta to make some high-voltage splices on the taxiways. I parked my car in the company parking lot that morning and drove one of the company trucks to Marietta and on to Dobbins Air Base. Those taxiways were still in use, and you had to be mindful at all times when an airplane might use them. On one occasion, I was sitting on the ditch bank adjacent to the taxiway. I had joint material, electric tape, sandpaper, cleaning fluid, and all the things necessary to make a splice. I had my back turned to the taxiway and the direction the planes would be coming in. Something told me to look around. One of the large military planes was coming at me about fifty yards behind. At first glance, it looked like the wing tips were almost touching the ground. I had to think fast, so I lay down on top of my splicing material. I knew that the back draft from those jet engines would blow my stuff everywhere. Thankfully, there was more room under those wing tips than I had first thought. The aircraft passed over me and began to move on down the taxiway toward the hangers. Just after the airplane passed over me, there was a great gush of wind from those jet engines. I did my best to protect my splicing material, but some of it blew back into the ditch anyway. From there on, I didn't turn my back to the taxiway for any thing. We worked for ten hours on that day, trying to get most of the work done. After our days work, I had to drive the company truck back to Atlanta and pick up my car. Upon reaching the company parking lot, I parked the truck in its place and got into my personal car.

The radio in my car immediately came on as I started my engine. The news broadcast that was being announced came as a great shock. The announcer said there had been a terrible explosion in the city of Villa Rica. There had been a number of people killed, and the Red Cross was on the scene. To say that I was shocked would be putting it mildly. I was renting a house in Villa Rica on East Wilson Street. The house was located just behind Richard's Motor Company, which was owned by Roy Richards, who also owned Southwire Company in Carrollton, Georgia. Mr. Holloway was the general manager of the business. Richard Smith and his brother Don pooled their resources and purchased the business in November 1970. That business still operates today in the city of Villa Rica.

My mother was living with us at the time of the explosion. I had two daughters, Dianne and Susanne, who were also at home that day. Neither of them was old enough to be in school. My wife, Edith, was working that day at the Sewell Manufacturing Company in Temple. There was a lady who helped through the week to see after our daughters while we were at work. Edith had told her that morning that she could take the girls downtown and let them look around for a while. Thank God, she did not do that.

As I listened to that news report on my car radio, I was going as fast as I dared to go to make my way home. I was very lucky to not be stopped by the police. When I got to Douglasville on Highway 78, there was a state patrolman standing at the red light. He said that the roads were blocked from there to Villa Rica to everyone, except emergency vehicles, and that I would not be allowed to go any further. I explained to him that I had a home there very near to the explosion sight. He then told me he was sorry, but he could not allow me to continue on that road. I said to him, "I will get there." I took a right turn onto Highway 92 toward Hiram, Georgia. About half way to Hiram, I turned west onto a road I was not familiar with. I kept winding my way around and finally came out at Buddy Stockmar's place. I knew where to go from there, so I made my way over to Highway 61. I was praying that the police did not have that road blocked. They did not, and I headed on into Villa Rica. When I arrived at the explosion sight, I could not believe my eyes. The drug store was the center point of the explosion. It was a two-story building with a dental office upstairs. There was a dress shop next to the drug store and a five-and-ten-cent store. What I saw was a deep hole in the ground. All the foundation walls were blown away. The building collapsed and burned. There were thirteen people killed in that explosion. Twelve were killed in the drug store and one, Rozelle Hammond, was killed in the five-and-ten-cent store. Had the explosion occurred thirty minutes later, the mill employees would have been in that building for lunch. I found out later what had happened. Bill Berry had called the Dyer Plumbing Company to come check out a gas smell in the building. He also called Oscar Hixon, who was in charge of the City of Villa Rica Gas Department. Mr. O.T. Dyer and his son, Johnny, were under the basement floor, trying to find the gas leak. They had been under there for some time when Mr. Hixon arrived at the drug store. Mr. Hixon proceeded to go to the basement and had about enough time to get down there when the explosion occurred.

There were several people in the drug store that survived the explosion. It must have been a horrible experience for them. The owner, Bill Berry, survived, but his wife, Margaret, did not. Ray Tyson, who had been an employee for a good long time, also survived. Another one or two survived, but together twelve did not. The names are as follows: Margaret Berry, Rob Broom, Dr. Jack Barnham, Carolyn Davis, Johnny Dyer, O. T. Dyer, Kenneth Hendrix, Oscar Hixon, Rozella Johnson, Bobby Roberts, Ann Pope Smith, and Carl Vinter. These names are listed on a plaque located across the street from the drug store.

I arrived at my home, which was only about two or three hundred yards from the explosion sight. I asked

Mama and the girls if they could hear or feel the explosion. They said the windows rattled, and the house jarred. I am so thankful my girls were not taken downtown that day. Edith was so very thankful as well. As she made her way home from her work in Temple, all she could think about was her children and their safety. She could not get a telephone to work, and she could not get any information or hear any news about what was going on or from her children. Thank God for his protecting hand.

In 1953, after being under conviction for some time, I came forward one Sunday morning to the altar in Fullerville Baptist Church and asked forgiveness for all my past sins and gave my life to God's service. Reverend Garland Odom was the preacher that Sunday morning. He was a powerful preacher of the Word and became a great friend of mine. Our firstborn child, Dianne, was two years old. Edith and I had been thinking we needed to get that child into some Christian training. What led me to my final decision was when Landrum Fendley, a fellow worker in the cotton mill, died of cancer. He was my wife's uncle, and we had become close friends after working together doffing twisters in the mill. I began to realize how close we all are to death. Cancer is a terrible disease, and Landrum suffered a lot before he died. Landrum said he was willing to suffer if it would bring Fullerville to its knees.

I joined Fullerville Baptist Church in 1953. It was a small church at that time. The auditorium was about forty-feet wide and fifty-feet long. There was no air conditioning. There were six Sunday school rooms attached to the back of the auditorium. Three of them were upstairs, and three were downstairs. A group of us men would get together some time later and build a dug out room downstairs. We opened a passage from the hallway to underneath the church. We then took pick, shovel, and a wheelbarrow to remove the dirt from underneath the auditorium. Once the dirt was removed, we ordered concrete and poured a floor for the room. Once the floor was finished, we could then start on the walls. We used volunteer workers to help with the work. One day, Steve was helping me with the work on the room. Steve was a good guy, but he was allergic to work. About mid-morning, he asked me if I would like to have something to drink and offered to go to the store to get some Cokes. I said yes, and he left for the store. He never came back. I understood because I knew his work habits. When the room was completed, we called it our prayer room. The men would meet together before a service, get down on the floor, and offer up their prayers. You could hear them throughout the other rooms. Everyone prayed at the same time. You could not detect one prayer from another, because all prayers were going up at the same time.

I had been a member for only one year when I was asked to be a deacon of Fullerville Baptist Church. That was in 1954. Ordination services back then were not shortcut services. There was an ordination sermon, a charge to the church, a charge to the candidate, and an ordination prayer. After all this, the candidate would kneel at the altar, and all the ordained men of the church would come around and lay hands on him. This could take some time, and your knees and legs would be very tired before they were through.

One of the men of the church was very strict in his

beliefs. Villa Rica had a public swimming pool. Edith and I would take our girls to the pool from time to time. It was a lot of fun and a good way to cool off from the summer heat. "Edgar" (not his real name) approached me one Sunday morning after the worship service and questioned me about taking my girls to the swimming pool. He asked me if I did not know that it was a sin to expose yourself in a bathing suit like that. My first instinct was to tell him to mind his own business, but I bit my tongue and let it pass. Some folks had some very funny beliefs. One man believed it was a sin to cut your fingernails on a Sunday. For a man to wear shorts was a no-no. You definitely were sinning if you played baseball on Sunday. Most of the men of the church were solid Christians and not carried away with these types of beliefs.

There were four benches on the platform with the pulpit. Two were on one side, and two were on the other side with the pulpit between the benches. Every preaching service, these four benches were full of deacons and some visiting preachers. The preacher would begin his sermon. He wouldn't go very far, until you could hear the men on the four benches shouting "*Amen*" almost in unison, followed by, "*Bless him, Lord.*" This could go on for almost his entire message. The church did not have a hired music man, so whoever was to lead the singing would lead a song and then call on several of the other men to come up and lead one. A few of the men would feel left out if they were not called on to lead a song. We had some very good trios and several singles, which were used from time-to-time.

The singing was spirit-filled and set a good tone for the preaching of the word.

In those early- to middle-fifties, we did not have a baptism pool in the church. Our baptismal services were held at different lakes from time to time. I was baptized at the Twin Lakes, here in Villa Rica. Several church members would gather at the water's edge for these services. After a couple of songs, the candidates would wade out in the water to about waist deep. The pastor would then baptize each candidate by putting them under the water and then raising them up out of the water. This was done according to the command of the Lord. Before the candidate was placed under the water the pastor would say, "In humble obedience to the great command of our Lord and Saviour Jesus Christ and upon your profession of faith in him, my brother or sister, I baptize you in the name of the Father, the Son, and The Holy Ghost." Baptism was a type of burying the old man who had died to the love and practice of sin in the liquid grave and raising him up to walk in the newness of life.

I was asked to teach the adult men and women's Sunday school class. I felt unworthy, because I had only been a member for about a year. After being persuaded by several members of the class, I agreed to give it a try. The mixed class of adults met in the auditorium of the church, because there was not a room large enough anywhere else in the church to meet. We did not use literature. All of our lessons were taken from the Bible. I started in Matthew, chapter one, and taught verse-by-verse, until the New Testament was completed through Revelation, the last chapter in the Bible. After going through the New Testament, I would go back to Matthew chapter one and start all over again. I don't know how many times I repeated this procedure, but I taught the adult men and women class for some twenty-five years. Occasionally, between finishing the New Testament, I would pick up a book of the Old Testament and teach it, before resuming my study in the New Testament. The first year that I taught the class, I felt so inadequate. On Saturday evening, I would make my way to the church. No one was there, and the door was never locked. I would go down to the dug-out prayer room and read my lesson for that Sunday. Before leaving to go back to my home, I would get down on that cement floor and lay flat out on my face with my Bible under my chest next to my heart. I would ask God to give me knowledge of his word. I am so thankful for those early years of Bible study.

The church began to grow, and it became evident we needed to enlarge our facility. We voted to build a new sanctuary and additional Sunday school rooms. Since I was an electrician, it fell on me to take care of that. The first thing I did with some voluntary help from some of the members was to enlarge our existing electrical service to where it would take care of the existing building plus a sub-feeder to our proposed new building. I never made a charge to the church for any of my time or labor. I felt like God had provided my vocation, and I was willing to give back to the Lord. We finished the new building, which was needed for our growth. The new auditorium was one hundred feet long and fifty-feet wide. Attached to and behind the auditorium were a number of Sunday school rooms. There was as much room under the church as there was upstairs. We had lots of rooms, a small kitchen, and enough room in the middle area for fellowship time. It took a lot of hours of my time to accomplish this task. My nephews, Richard and John Wayne, were faithful to help me most of the time. Other volunteers helped, and when we needed them the most, they would show up.

I had finished my days work in Atlanta and was driving home on Bankhead Highway, when I saw "Edgar" (not his real name), standing on the sidewalk. He was waiting for a bus to pick him up. I asked him if he wanted a ride home. He said he did and got into my car beside me. Traffic was really busy that day, and it was just stop and go. I asked Edgar where he had been, and he said he had been for a job interview. I asked him how he had done with the interview. He was an uneducated man and sometimes would extend the truth. He said they had sat him down at a typewriter and that he had typed one hundred and twenty words a minute. I knew this was an untruth, because I knew his educational background and that he probably did not know how to type.

I said, "Well, Edgar, did you get the job?" He said he did not and couldn't imagine why he didn't. Walking down the sidewalk, there was a scantly clad, good-looking girl. There was a big truck behind my car. The truck driver couldn't take his eyes off the girl. In this stop and go traffic, I stopped, and the truck driver failed to stop. He later told me he was not looking at me but had his eyes on the young girl. When his truck struck my little Ford car, it jarred us pretty hard. Edgar blatted out a curse word. I looked over at him and thought, *Is this the same man who thought it was wrong for me to take my daughters to the swimming pool?* There are a lot of people who talk the talk, but do not walk the walk.

I saw a lot of people come and go in the church. Some thought they could come and just take a little dose of "do better and everything would be all right." But it does not work that way. Someone with whom I used to play ball came one revival night and said he gave his life to the Lord. I knew him very well and was glad to see him make the move. He was really in to it for a number of weeks, before his true character came out. During those several weeks, he was even considered by some of the men as a candidate for the deacon ministry. I knew of his old habits of wine, women, and song. I let the truth run its course, and it was not very long until he was right back into the hog pen. What makes a hog wallow in the mire? Because there is something about it they like. What makes a dog return again to its vomit? Because there is something about it they like. Some people look at a fallen man like that and call all church people hypocrites. In this case, he had never really surrendered himself to the Lord's service. When the temptations began to come back to him, he did not have the spirit to help him. He later would die an untimely death.

After I joined Fullerville Baptist Church, I became very close to Slick Odum. We had always been good friends, but the friendship became closer because of our church activities together. Slick was a great fisherman. He knew all there was to know about bass fishing. I had never fished on a serious note until he took me under his wings. After fishing with Slick for some time, I began to love the sport. I bought all I needed to fish with: new rod and reels, all kind of lures, plastic worms, tackle box, and so forth. I did not own a boat, but Slick invited me to go with him most of the time. Sometimes we would plan a trip to Lake Lanier. It was a great fishing lake. It was quite a distance from Villa Rica to Lake Lanier, so sometimes we would leave home about two o'clock in the morning to get there. I would set my clock to wake me up, but it was not really necessary, because I could hardly sleep in great anticipation of our fishing trip. We would leave Villa Rica at two o'clock in the morning, go up to about Cartersville, and stop at a restaurant to eat breakfast. We then would make our way on up to Cumming near to Six-Mile Creek. We would back Slick's boat up to a boat ramp and slide it off into the water. We would park our car and get into the boat. The moment first light hit the water we would be on our way. We would make our way with a gasoline engine to one of his favorite coves. We then would shut the gasoline engine down and use the scull on the other side of the boat. We would ease the boat around the cove staying, about twenty-five yards from the bank and cast our lines toward the bank. You have never lived until you have cast a top water tiny torpedo plug out on the water that early in the morning. The water is as smooth as glass. As you make a gentle pull on the line to get action from the fishing lure, suddenly it seems as though the lake has exploded under your lure. You jerk back on the line and feel the weight on the other end of the line. The reel sings as you turn the wheel. After a moment or two, the fish jumps up out of the water, trying to throw the lure from his mouth. You continue to reel him in. As he gets close to the boat, Slick grabs the dip net and reaches down into the water with it. When he comes up with the dip net, there is a three pound bass in the net. There is no experience greater than that. As you place the fish on the stringer, your heart begins to pound.

Ollie and Bud Oak were two young men of Fullerville who also loved to fish. They were fishing together one morning at the Legion Lake in Villa Rica. Ollie had thrown a tiny torpedo out into the water. A bass made a pass at the lure, and Ollie jerked back on the line. The lure became airborne and was flying back toward the boat. Bud Oak did not have time to duck, and the lure caught him on the head between his eyes. It stuck there, and they had to go to the doctor to get the lure cut out of his head. That was a funny sight, as Bud Oak walked into the doctor's clinic with a tiny torpedo stuck in his head.

Another story Ollie told and swore it was true was about him and Bud Oak fishing there at Legion Lake. They had gone about forty yards off the shore when Ollie cast his line out with a plastic worm attached to it. He felt a hit on the line and set the hook. He felt the load on the line and began reeling in. As he got the fish close to the boat, he told Bud Oak to get the dip net. Bud Oak dropped the dip net into the water and felt a thud in the net. He raised the dip net up, and he had a two- pound catfish in the net. Ollie was still reeling in the fish on his line. Bud Oak dropped the catfish into the boat. He then reached back into the water with the dip net and came up with a bass on Ollie's line. The only explanation was that the bass had excited the catfish and was running through the water at the right time.

I fished for several years, until one day I asked Edith about us buying our own boat. She said she didn't think we could afford one at this time. Of course, she was right. But I was tired of going when some one else wanted to go and not exactly when I wanted to go. I said, "I quit fishing."

The next weekend I made my way to Rockmart, Georgia, and to the Goodyear Golf Club. I bought a used set of golf clubs for one hundred dollars. This began a long journey for me at the sport of golf. A group of us from Villa Rica joined the Goodyear Golf Club, which had only nine holes. We would all gather together on the weekend at the first tee box and make up our foursomes. Then, for a couple of dollars at stake, you would think we were playing the U.S. Open. It was a fun time for all those who played.

I first became involved with golf as a teenager. On a Saturday, I would hitchhike from Villa Rica to Lithia Springs. The Suggs family owned the golf course there. You may recall Louise Suggs, who played on the women's professional golf tour. After arriving at the golf course, I would rent a set of golf clubs for three dollars. I paid two dollars for green fee, and I was ready to go. You could buy golf balls for twenty-five to fifty cents each. I never had any training with my golf game. All I knew how to do, as John Daley said, was to grip it and rip it. Consequently,

I never became a low handicap golfer; however, I always enjoyed playing the game.

Our group played at Goodyear Golf Club until Fairfield Plantation golf course opened up. Westinghouse Corporation purchased land near Sandhill between Villa Rica and Carrollton. They sold lots for homes and built a golf course with a swimming pool and tennis court. There was a fishing lake and recreation lake, and other things were offered. Donald Gibson and I went in together and bought a lot of land. This gave us the opportunity to join the golf club. That worked out really good for a lot of years. I learned more about golf there than I ever learned before. Charles Sorrell was the golf pro there for some time. I purchased a set of Ping clubs from him, and I still have them to this day. He worked with me on my game and did much to help me improve. He is a great teacher of the golf game, and I respect him very much.

Before Interstate 20 West was opened for traffic, it was necessary to travel Highway 78 to Atlanta. Traffic in those early morning trips to work was very crowded, to say the least. Sometimes we would go Campbelton Road and Cascade Road as an alternative route. Two lane highways made it very difficult to pass, and sometimes when running late, we would take chances we shouldn't take. Fortunately, we never had a serious accident. However, in my thirty-nine years of traveling back and forth, I witnessed a number of very serious accidents. One that was kind of comical was on our way home out Cascade way. A driver had spun out, and his car had come to rest in a deep ditch. The driver's door had somehow come open, and the car had the driver's leg pinned against a dirt bank. He could not get out, because the weight of the car kept him pinned in. I ran over to the car to see if I could help. He said someone had already called for help. He had a pint of white whiskey with him, which was about half used up. He asked me to take the whiskey and hide it in the woods adjacent to his car. He didn't want the law to see the whiskey. He said he would retrieve it later. I felt sorry for him, took the whiskey bottle, and put it in the woods as he asked, but I put it so he would not be able to find it. He thought more of his whiskey than he did for his leg that was pinned against the bank.

We were traveling Highway 78 toward home one evening and had passed Lithia Springs about a mile back when we came upon a head-on collision. Both cars were terribly mangled, and both drivers were laid out on the highway, but still alive. Charles knew one of the drivers and ran over to him. The collision had taken most of the skin off his chin area, and you could see bone. He wanted Charles to pick him up, but Charles would not do it. He could have caused further injury if he tried to pick him up. He became very angry, because we would not help him up and began to curse. We could do nothing but wait for proper medics to get there. The other driver was hurt very badly, but we did not know him. All I remember about him was that he was having a hard time keeping his false teeth in his mouth. I never heard the outcome of their condition.

You never know what you might see on the highway.

One day, Matt and I were going west on I-20 toward home. I constantly look in my rearview mirror as I drive, and the traffic was busy that evening on all lanes of the highway. As I looked in my rear view mirror, I could see a vehicle approaching at a very fast speed in the left lane in which I was driving. I immediately moved over into the middle lane, but the cars in front of me did not move over. The approaching vehicle was frantically trying to get by. He took the emergency lane and began to pass everyone on the left side of the road. I knew immediately why when I saw a Georgia State Patrol car on his tail with the blue light flashing and his siren going. We had just passed the crest of the hill, and I had a clear view of the following events. It was like we were sitting in a drive-in movie. The sports car reached the bottom of the hill and suddenly turned left across the median in his attempt to escape the officer. What he did not know was that an unmarked law vehicle was sitting on the other side of the road. The sports car crossed over into the other highway, but with his high speed, he ran headfirst into the guardrail. The unmarked vehicle closed in on him on his right side, and the patrol car closed in on him on his left side. I thought to myself, you are caught now. I just didn't know how desperate the driver of the sports car was. Suddenly, the officers got out of their vehicles with their guns drawn. The driver of the sports car suddenly backed out between the two officers' cars and started to cross back over the median of the highway. At this point, the state patrol officer began firing his revolver at the sports car. The driver, fearing for his life I suppose, stopped his vehicle and got out with his hands in the air. The officers then subdued the driver and handcuffed him. He was then placed into the patrol car. It was like going to a movie and not having to buy a ticket.

While driving an automobile back and forth from Villa Rica to Atlanta, there was always something happening. One of my early morning trips to Atlanta was a good example of what could happen to you. I was driving my pick-up truck, and I had just passed the Thornton Road exit and had made my way up to the next long hill. Upon reaching the crest of this hill, you can see Atlanta in the distance. I was then—and I still am—amazed at the size the city had become. Suddenly, the left front tire on my pick-up truck blew out. I was traveling in the left lane next to the concrete wall. I was forced to move into the emergency lane next to the concrete wall. I sat there for a minute or two, trying to decide what to do. Since the flat was on the side next to the wall, I decided to try to change the tire myself. I retrieved the jack and the tire tools from under the passenger side of the truck. I then slipped around to the back of the truck and lowered the spare tire from underneath the truck bed. I then lay down on the ground to see where to put the jack, so I could jack the truck up and remove the old tire. All the time traffic was whizzing by. As I lay there on the ground, I looked back in the direction the traffic was coming from, and I could see those headlights as they crossed over the crest of the hill. As they passed my truck, I could feel the truck jar because of the wind from the passing vehicles. I prayed, "Lord, if I am going to die here, please let it be quick." I heard a voice saying, "Can I help you?" It was a coworker of mine who had seen me, had driven to the next exit, and circled back. He parked next to the wall on the opposite side and stood up on his truck. I thought at first it was an angel. I replied to him, "No, I am about done now, but I thank you anyway." I tightened the lugs back on the wheel and threw all the tools and the blown-out tire into the truck bed. I was never as happy in my life as I was when I sat down in my truck when I was through. I waited for my lane to clear and got back on the highway. One of the greatest blessings of retirement was getting off the interstate highway.

I was doing an electrical job in Cedartown at a chemical company. The work was to install wiring around an oxidation pond. This involved setting poles around the pond and stringing wire. We set disconnect switches at various locations around the pond. I left Atlanta with the boom truck to which was attached a pole trailer. I had five poles strapped to the pole trailer. The boom truck was getting on in miles and age. It was not a fun thing to drive from Atlanta to Cedartown. Traffic would pile up behind the truck. Needless to say, they were frustrated, as well as me. I would find a spot where I could get over, wait until traffic cleared, and then resume the trip. I finally arrived in Cedartown after a two-and-a-half hour trip. I pulled into the pond area and disconnected the pole trailer from the boom truck. I breathed a sigh of relief as I parked the boom truck near the pond. It had been a rainy season, and the area around the pond was a sloppy mess. I knew we would need a mud hog type of truck to handle the work. I had seen a group of linemen working on the side of the road. I decided to go and talk to them about doing the setting of the poles and stringing the wire on a subcontract basis. We agreed on a price, and the next weekend, they came in, set the poles, and strung the wire. I was glad to get that much done, because my boom truck would have never made it through that muddy mess. While doing that job, I drove a company truck back and forth from Villa Rica to Cedartown.

While going home from work one evening just south of Cedartown on Highway 27, a strange thing happened. I was following an eighteen-wheeler. We were in a zone where you shouldn't pass. Suddenly a car, driven by a lady, passed me and the eighteen-wheeler. She completed her passing and looked as though she was pulling in front of the truck to resume down the road. While pulling in front of the truck, she never did straighten back in the road but ran directly in to a very deep ditch next to a driveway. Her vehicle hit head on with the bank on the other side of the ditch. She didn't have a seat belt on, and it was evident she was very seriously injured. Her face had hit directly into something in the car. We got word the next day that she had died that evening in the hospital.

As I close this book, I will never forget Fullerville and the men and women who made up that mill village. As I pass through there from time to time, I still recall names and faces of most all the folks who made up that mill village. There was Waldrop's café, Grubbs barber shop, Florence's Grocery Store (later to become the pool hall), Charlie

Bilbo's place, Hamrick's Grocery Store, and the Fullerville Ball Park. I remember the old oak tree where the workers would come out for a break and tell their favorite tales. Some were true, and some were not so true. I remember the one-room courthouse and the old cement jailhouse. It still sits there today as a reminder of times past. I remember my wife's papa, Mr. Ben Rast, who was police chief for a number of years. Mr. Fuller would take over the police job, after Mr. Rast gave it up. I remember climbing the water tank at the cotton mill many times. I don't know how I got out of there alive. I can still hear the whistle of my brother, Cecil, as he could do his lips a certain way and make a loud, whistling sound. This was to tell the workers to come in from the old tree and get back to work. I remember Oree's mustard and egg sandwiches I brought her each day. I remember Aunt Pearl's eggs and milk I carried to her each day.

We didn't know we were poor folks. We just had a good time with what we had. Some of the sacrifices I had to make made me a better person. I know how to be in want, and I know how to be full. I just want to say thank you to the good Lord for allowing me to be a part of the history of Fullerville.